Your Family Legacy

Learn How to Create a Cherished Gift and Use Your New Skill to Build a Lucrative Business

By

I0423028

Karen J Cornwell

Feelings of worth can flourish only in an atmosphere where individual differences are appreciated, mistakes are tolerated, communication is open, and rules are flexible - the kind of atmosphere that is found in a nurturing family. ~ Virginia Satir

Contents

Keep away from people who try to belittle your ambitions.

Small people always do that; but the really great ones make you feel that you too, can become great.

~ Mark Twain

Creating Your Family Legacy

Introduction

In this book you will find a unique way to record your own family memories, the easiest way to help someone else record their family memories and there is also a section that will show you how to create a lucrative business from your new-found skills.

The book contains all the practical information you will need to implement all the methods suggested.

This book does not show you how to conduct a genealogy search nor does it show you how to construct a family tree but, for those who have already collated that information, it will show you how to put all your information together in a published book.

I first began to use this system and build my business after discovering a .pdf from a fellow writer. She wrote:

"*It occurred to me that there are things about my grandparents who have passed away that I will never know. That led to me wondering if there are things in my own parents life that I would love to record for posterity; some way of documenting their memories for future generations.*

So, I decided to create something that would be a legacy – not just for my children, but for other family members as well.

Oh, I know that you can buy books that ask the questions and you can write the answers in the book so that you can create your own biography.

*Whilst that is a great idea for some, I wanted to go a step further – I wanted a **real book, professionally bound and published,** where I could purchase copies to give to the family members who were interested, and others could also buy copies if they wanted to…*"

I had already self-published quite a few of my own books and thought that this would be the ideal way to create my own family legacy.

So I came up with some simple questions for my parents and I interviewed them.

That was my first foray into the world of self-publishing for others and the catalyst for my thriving business.

You could use the information in this book to create and publish your own books easily and cheaply.

There are an ever increasing number of people who are researching their family tree. What better way to preserve that family research than putting it all together in a beautiful book.

However, this is something that I also used to create a very nice income and you could too; once you have learned the process of self-publishing.

I run workshops teaching people how to implement this technique to create a Family Legacy for themselves.

I teach how to conduct the interview with their family member, how to edit and format for publication and how to create a book cover before uploading to Createspace.

For those who are interested I also teach how to upload their work to Amazon Kindle.

This means that purchasers can download the books to read with any e-book reader.

It is a very simple process and only takes a short time to learn how to do this and adds extra value to your workshops.

See later in this book for instructions.

More about the workshops later...

A lot of people who purchase this book simply want to know how they can create their own memorable legacy to leave for their family so their life story will be permanently recorded for posterity.

Others may want to involve a lot of their family members so that each can contribute their own memories.

Or maybe someone would want to record the memories of an older family member who may not be able to do this for themselves.

Whatever your plans, creating a beautifully printed and bound book of your Family Legacy is a great way to preserve memories for future generations that may otherwise be forgotten.

Your Family Legacy

A simple way to create *your own personal* Family Legacy is to use the sample questions included later in the book as a guide and write a few paragraphs (or more...) answering each question.

Then follow the self-publishing instructions for formatting, creating a cover and uploading for publication.

To Create a Family Legacy for someone else ('client') follow the steps below

You will need:

- Two methods of recording the interview
- A list of question suggestions to help prompt your client
- A quiet place to conduct the interview
- *At the very least* two hours to get the material recorded
- A contact to be signed by both parties.

When you have all the material collected you will need:

- The Self-Publishing instructions (see section 2 of this book) to guide you through the formatting and publishing process

Conducting the Interview

Make sure that you bring something to record the interview with. Remember to bring extra batteries. If possible, bring two items to record with in case the first one fails – for example, bring a dictaphone and a camcorder.

It would be awful if you spent a couple of hours getting some great information only to find that you haven't got it recorded...

SO CHECK THAT YOUR RECORDING EQUIPMENT IS IN GOOD WORKING ORDER BEFORE YOU START

If you have speech to text software like Dragon Naturally Speaking it will make your job so much easier. Simply set up your interviewee with a microphone and ask your questions.

The words should appear on your screen and you can take away the laptop and edit it later. It may take a little longer to edit because you will have to insert punctuation etc.

You also have to remember that the software does not always get it right, so you have to check for mistakes i.e 'to' instead of 'two' etc.

But it is so much quicker than having to transcribe the whole interview. Remember, whatever recording system you are using always use two methods to record the interview as stated above – just in case...

NOTE: Dragon Naturally Speaking (available on Amazon) is only useful if you are just interviewing one client. If there are a few people involved, other methods of recording the interview will be required.

Make sure you choose a place that is comfortable, quiet and without outside distractions.

It helps with scheduling if you arrange to go to your client's house; they will be more comfortable and relaxed.

Make sure you have everything you will need before you go; notebook, pens, recording equipment, contact etc.

There may be times when you ask a question and the person you are interviewing may not remember or may not have a quick answer – don't pressure the person to answer, especially if you are interviewing someone who is older. They may have a memory issue, and you don't want to upset them. Remember, this is supposed to be a fun experience for everyone involved.

There may be times when you ask a question and it may seem to you that the person being interviewed is saddened or upset. Be sure to ask if they want to stop and take a break.

Ask if the interviewee would like to have another person sit in to help the conversation flow.

Sometimes having a close relative or friend to prompt the interviewee with reminders such as, "remember when you..." helps to jog the memory.

On the other hand, sometimes that can limit the amount of information that you can get because the interviewee may be reluctant to reveal some things in front of a third person. There may be things that they want to include in their book so other people can it read at a later date.

Let your client make the final decision.

Some people may want to make this a family experience by gathering as many family members together as they can so that everyone can contribute to their personal Family Legacy.

In my experience this approach can get a bit chaotic and turn into a family nostalgia meeting, but it can also be a lot of fun. Your job is to keep the conversation on track so that you can get the information for the book in as short a time as possible – your time is money!

Another way of creating a book that includes memories from multiple contributors is by asking each potential participant to write down their contribution and maybe supply photographs for inclusion in the book. The client (the one paying your fee) would then make the decision of the material they want to include in their book.

Be sympathetic and patient at all times. There may be memories that your client wants to include that are painful to remember – the loss of a loved one, a marriage breakup etc.

Make sure that you have **at least** two hours for the first interview.

Depending on the client's story, you may have to schedule further meetings to get the material that you need to create their book.

Be sure to schedule breaks – but if things are going well, don't interrupt and break the flow. Wait until there is a natural stopping point.

Once you have finished asking all your questions, always ask if there is anything else that the interviewee would like to add.

There may be a special memory that you didn't know about and that wasn't covered by your question and answer approach.

Before your first meeting, get your client to collect any photographs they would like to have in their book. Ask them to put them in chronological order to make thing simpler.

Having these to hand can also help the first interview progress. You could go through the photographs together whilst the client talks about each one.

If there will be a lot of photos involved, you may want to buy a cheap album or some transparent wallets as you will have to take the photos away to scan them into your computer.

You will also be able to make notes on the album or wallet regarding the positioning of the photos in the finished book.

Basic Interview Progression

Keep in mind that every interview is going to be different.

One of the reasons you are recording the interview is so that you can focus less on asking questions and getting answers and more on listening and interacting with the person that you are interviewing.

Whilst the question and answer methods works well, some people just like to chat about their life and that is fine.

In fact it is sometimes better than asking questions – you should be able to get everything that you need for a great Family Legacy by simply leading the client in the right direction during your 'chat'.
The sample questions that are given in the next section are simply a starting point.

You don't have to ask every single question.

You also are not limited to the questions that are given as sometimes the interview takes on a direction of its own and you should just go with the flow.

If the person you are interviewing gives any vague answers or gives an answer that you would like to know more about, ask a

follow-up question to clarify and expand the topic.
Spontaneity is fine as long as you are able to 'lead' your client in the right direction.
The basic interview should cover what any biography would:

- History about their parents

- Early childhood memories

- Adolescence and teenage years

- Any firsts that they have – first sleepover, first broken bone, first date, first day of school, etc.

- Childhood and high school friends

- Primary school, high school, and college

- First job – pay, conditions etc.

- Any special memories

- Achievements

- Their partner or spouse

- Children

- Progressing to the present day

But of course, as you are providing a service for the client, they get to decide what they want to have included in their book.

There are times when the person you are interviewing may skip around, and that's fine.

You can always organize everything later as long as you have it recorded.

Details are always a nice thing and they also help put things in perspective. I'll give you a couple of examples

Fuel prices

Times when you have an interviewee talk about how petrol was only 25p a *gallon* and they thought that it was outrageous at that price.

Bread prices

A loaf of sliced bread cost around one shilling (5p) in the early sixties.

Note: These are UK prices but you get the idea...

Ask for a few examples of prices of things from your clients experience to include in the book. It really does help to create a mental image about what their life at that time was like and may trigger other memories of that time.

Some Question Ideas

This is not an exhaustive list, and you do not have to use all of the questions. Some of the questions will not apply to everyone, so you must use your judgement to decide which questions are appropriate for your subject. The questions are really just used to prompt the client if they get stuck in recalling their experiences.

1. What were your parents like when you were growing up?

2. What were their jobs?

3. How did your parents meet?

4. How long were they married before you were born?

5. How many brothers and sisters you have?
   - Are they older than you?
   - Younger?

6. How did you get on with your siblings when you were growing up?

7. What is your first childhood memory?

8. What was your favourite food when you were a child?

9. Describe the first childhood home that you remember.

10. What were your favourite games to play when you were a child?

11. What were some of your friends names when you were a child?

12. Who was your best friend when you were a child?

13. Did you have a pet?

14. What are some family traditions that you remember?

15. What was your favourite holiday when you were growing up?

16. What was your first day of school like?

17. What were your favourite subjects in school?

18. What are some activities you enjoyed doing when you were in primary school? High school?

19. Describe some of your memories of school
    - favourite subjects,
    - favourite teachers,
    - best friends,
    - boyfriends/girlfriends,
    - things you used to do when you were hanging out after school

20. Did you enjoy school?

21. What were your favourite extracurricular activities when you were in school?

22. What did you do during the school holidays?

23. If you could go back and change one thing that you did in school, what would it be?

24. If you could go back and talk to one teacher that you had in school, who would it be and what would you tell him or her?

25. What was your first job?

26. How much was your first pay cheque?

27. What did you spend it on?

28. How did you meet your spouse?

29. How did you know that that person was going to be the one that you married?

30. What was your wedding day like?

31. What was your honeymoon like?

32. What was that first year of marriage like?

33. What would you have done differently?

34. What did you wish that you knew before you got married?

35. What about your children?

36. Do you remember finding out when you were going to have a child?
    - what was your reaction?
    - what was your spouse's reaction?
    - talk about how you felt

37. How did it feel the day you became a parent?

38. If you could go back and re-live one day – what would it be? What would you do differently, if anything?

39. How different from today was it bringing up children when your   children were small?

40. If you could go back and change one thing in your life, what would it be?

41. What is your happiest memory?

42. What piece of advice would you leave for your children and/or grandchildren?

Before concluding the interview remember to ask if there is anything else that they would like to chat about – this is the time when I usually get the best content.

The client seems to switch off from 'interview' mode and goes into 'chat' mode, telling me all sorts of things that I had not even thought about asking. So when setting your schedule, always allocate a little extra time at the end of each interview for a 'chat' and keep recording.

If you are creating a Family Legacy for a paying client, you should schedule a brief meeting after each stage of the book creation to make absolutely sure that your client is happy with how the process is going.

These are the stages involved:

1) Recording the memories. Meet (or call) with the client after the recording to make sure they are happy with how things went.

It may take more than one session to get all the information – each interview is different.

2) Transcribing the recording for print. Send a copy of the interview for their perusal.

Ask the client if there is anything else that they would like to add after they have read the first draft.

3) Choosing a title for the book.

It is very important for the client to be involved in this.

4) Formatting the interior pages with their name as author.

Show the client the draft .pdf to make sure that they are happy with the content before you submit it for publication. Get the client to sign a copy of the .pdf to say that they approve of the content and that you have their permission to go ahead with publication.

5) Creating a book cover.

Let the client choose colours and any photographs for the cover etc.

6) Setting up a publishers account so they can receive royalties on any sales (if they want to have the finished book on sale).

7) Uploading for print.

Email or call the client to tell them that the book has been submitted for publication.

8) Checking the finished proof copy.

After you have read the first proof copy, have your client look it over to make sure they are still happy with the content.

9) Delivering five copies of the published book.

Remind your client that this is not an overnight process as there is a lot of preparation involved.

ALWAYS take a deposit from the client with the balance to be paid in agreed stages to minimise your risk.

Create a simple working agreement to give to your client so there will be no 'misunderstandings' and everyone is clear about the process and costs involved.

Have two copies signed by you both, one for your records and one for the client.

Things you could include:

1) The price of the complete service.

I have a scale of charges depending on the finished length of the book otherwise you could end up writing a 'War and Peace' tome for the same price as a booklet sized book.

2) An approximate timescale but do stress that this is only a guide as the process varies with each client. Some clients require more than one initial meeting to collect the material.

3) A schedule of non-refundable part payments at intervals throughout the process.

It would be awful to get halfway through and the client decides that they don't want the book after all.

At least if you get a deposit to cover time spent collecting their material and transcribing it for print and perhaps a payment after they have seen the draft copy, you will not have worked for nothing if they change their mind.

4) Any extras that you think could come up.

It may be sensible to have a Lawyer draw up or look over your working agreement to make sure that the legalities are taken care of.

Section 1a

The Workshops

The workshops alone make me a very nice income and it means that I can work when I choose to.

The workshops teaching the whole Family Legacy and self-publishing method (see Publishing section for full details) are ideal to promote to creative writers groups. Most of the participants in these groups dream of having their work in print and most would not know about this simple and cheap way of self-publishing their own books.

You can show them how to fulfil this dream for very little outlay.

From poetry to full length novels; it can all be done using this method.

Another great place to promote your workshops is your local women's groups or your local church (for fundraising books) and you could also visit the local care homes for the elderly (for Family Legacy books).

The workshops are great places for new ideas.

For instance, the ladies circle that I met with recently at one of my workshops decided that they would like to create a local recipe book for a fundraising drive.

They asked their members and other locals for a family recipe, along with a paragraph or two and maybe a photograph telling why this was a family favourite, to include in the book. The ladies chose the ones that they wanted to include, then published the recipe book to sell for a profit to put towards their funds.

The local church group hit on the idea of publishing a history of the parish with contributions from anyone with local memories that they wanted to share. They asked for old photographs of the locality with a paragraph or two describing the scene and its relevance to the contributor.

I got the job of formatting and publishing both of these books. They simply collected the material (the most time consuming part...) and handed it over to me. A couple of weeks later I presented them with 5 books for their approval. They were thrilled.

I show my workshop attendees how to create a great Christmas or birthday gift for children. I, or the purchaser, write a short story including all the child's friends, family and pets. The child is the hero of the unique story which is based around their age and their own particular interests.

I include lots of photographs supplied by the purchaser and the child's photo is on the front cover of the book.

The purchaser is always listed as the author whoever wrote the content.

You can also show people how to get their music or movies published for distribution on Createspace, giving you a whole lot more people to market your workshops to.

I find that some of the workshop attendees would much rather have someone else write, format and upload their Family Legacy book for them, so I offer that service as well.

I put up posters advertising this service.

If you do decide to go down the road of writing a whole Family Legacy for someone, always calculate your time accurately and charge accordingly.

Remember you are offering a unique service that not many other people will be able to offer.

For those of you who intend to use this information to create a lucrative workshop business, you have my permission to use any of the copy and information contained in this book to create your workshop material.

You could even run this business entirely online.

Set up a comprehensive questionnaire and email it to your client.

Follow the same steps as for the 'face to face' method using email for the follow up after each step in the book creation process as outlined previously.

You can teach this process in one 2 to 3 hour workshop or spread it out over two meetings.

But don't be tempted to use two meetings full of waffle if you can fit the information into one meeting – people don't appreciate spending their money and time if they don't leave your workshops with some actionable information.

After preparing the material for the first workshop you can use this for each subsequent one.

You will need to issue every attendee with a brief outline or checklist of the process for collecting the information for their book for future reference.

The information should be general, not specific for a particular type of book because people will form different plans as a result of what they will learn from you.

Some will want to go down the route of the Family Legacy (which is what you will promote when you advertise), others may want to create a local recipe book or a collection of poems etc.

You could also reproduce the Family Legacy questions page of this book and include this in your course material. If you think of any more questions – add those too.

The other important thing that you need to give to your attendees is the Publishing instructions included in this book so they have a reference when formatting their own book.

To add extra value, you could distribute a Kindle publishing guide (see later in this book) to each of your attendees.

The Publishing Guide section is a step-by-step guide to the formatting and publishing process using Createspace.

Alternatively, you could research the process involved using Lulu.com, another self-publishing platform. Lulu.com have a great template for self-publishing family photographs in a printed and bound book (another idea to teach in your workshops).

At my workshops I usually show how to create a 21st birthday, wedding gift or significant anniversary gift using the Lulu photograph book.

Once you have all your materials prepared for your workshops the next step is to practise your presentation.

Create a PowerPoint presentation for your workshop – it's much easier to 'show' rather than 'tell'. Most venues have a PowerPoint projector that you can hire for your presentation just in case a venue doesn't have one for hire.

When you have run a few successful workshops you may want to consider buying your own projector from the proceeds. Until you have your own projector you are limited to venues that can supply one.

It is a good idea to get a few friends or family members together to act as your first 'audience'.

It is important to time the presentation so you know how long it will take you to get the information across but remember to add some time at the end for questions.

During your presentation be natural; like you are chatting to friends, but try and keep your audience on track and not allow them to wander too far off the topic. Treat the rehearsal as the real thing.

Encouraging chat is good as people can come up with ideas that you may not have considered before but it is your job to control the direction of the chat to avoid your presentation going on for too long.

I usually work within 100 miles of my home and am lucky to have lots of venues available to hold my workshops.

On a couple of occasions I have been asked to travel further afield to conduct a workshop (yes, I do get requests to present this interesting workshop...), but when I do, I always remember to factor in my increased costs (extra time travelling and fuel costs) when setting a price per attendee.

I advertise in local free ad papers, on church noticeboards and on community noticeboards.

I also contact the local (to the venue) newspaper well in advance, with a press release about my service to see if they will be prepared to run it in their paper.

The concept is unusual enough to get quite a lot of free advertising. I have contacted the local radio stations but not had much luck there – it may be different in your area though.

I started off my business with some great FREE advertising by holding a competition in conjunction with my local paper. The entrants had to submit a piece not longer than 300 words saying why they should have a book published about their life or family.

The editor and I read all the entrants and chose a winner. I then did that book for free. By doing this I was also able to calculate how long the process would take and it gave me a good idea how much to charge for subsequent clients.

In the copy for the competition I outlined my new business; the workshops, the children's gift books and the complete book writing service. This was the way I filled my first workshop and I also picked up three clients for the complete book writing service.

So the one free book that I did for the competition as a loss leader, really jump started my business and also gave me an idea of the time involved when working for an individual client. So I was able to structure my pricing more accurately.

I really hope that you will be able to make good use of this information to build yourself a lucrative business. You will probably be able to come up with some variations of your own based on the general idea if you do a bit of 'brainstorming'.

One last thing regarding the Family Legacy or Workshop business - **Always Provide Excellent Value for Your Clients.**

If they like your product they will tell others but they will also tell others if they feel they haven't got value for money.

This is a very unique and lucrative business if you just get out there and do it.

Take the bull by the horns and really 'go for it' – this could be your ticket to a great business that you can run at your own pace.

Just think, no more having to get up and drag yourself to the office – you run your business in your own time; you work when you want to and be proud that you can offer this unique service to your clients.

Please keep me informed of your success – I always love to hear of anyone who can take full control of their own destiny...

If there is anything that I can help you with, please feel free to email me – I will usually be able to respond within 48 hours.

ljs@iwantd.com

PLEASE NOTE: The following pages are excerpts from other books that I have previously published online as digital books. So please view them as separate sections that are necessary to the "Your Family Legacy" business model.

Section 2

Self-Publishing – the Easy Way

Introduction

Have you got a manuscript or two sitting in a drawer with rejection slips attached?

Have you tried to get an agent or publisher interested and not had much luck?

These days agents and publishers are inundated with manuscripts and there are only a very few authors that manage to get published. Even if you are offered a deal it may be anything up to a year before your book is finally ready for distribution.

What if I could show you a way to get your book published and available on Amazon within a WEEK or so – and all for the price of your proof copy (around $4 + postage)?

Would you be interested?

Of course you would…

This method requires a little knowledge of uploading files to a website but that is the only technical knowledge that you will require, everything else will be laid out for you in the following pages.

If you struggle with uploading files, ask someone to show you how. Once you have done it a few times, it is really very simple.

The Publisher

There are a lot of print-on-demand publishers available but the one that I use most is www.Createspace.com. They make it very simple to get your books in print.

They are a subsidiary of Amazon which is why you can get your books onto Amazon's list in less than a week after approving your proof copy.

The other great benefit of using Createspace to self-publish your book is that it is very easy to do and it is FREE – apart from the cost of your proof copy + shipping.

You can publish anything from a huge tome of a novel to a 24 page booklet; whatever you want to write about can be published.

Heck, your children could write their very own book and see it in print within a few weeks. I published a collection of my Granddaughters poems as a Christmas gift. She was thrilled to be a published author at 10 years old.

The first thing to remember is that this particular publisher will only publish *exactly* what you send them.

They will not do any proofreading, editing or formatting at all.

So you need to format your pages correctly (I'll show you how…) and proofread it yourself or get someone else to have a look over it for you.

I usually finish a book, proofread and edit it once, then put it away for a week or so before doing the same again. I also get someone else to go through it for obvious spelling and grammar mistakes.

It is amazing the simple mistakes that you will pick up after reading through a second time. There is nothing more frustrating than receiving your proof copy, only to find a very basic grammar or spelling error.

The first step, after you have written your book is to:

Sign up at Createspace

Visit the website www.createspace.com and sign up for a free account.

Simply follow the step-by-step process – it only takes a few minutes.

Royalties

If you are publishing a book that you want to sell commercially, have a look around the Createspace website. You will see a section that will calculate the potential royalties for you.

The beauty of Createspace is that you can publish anything as just a 'one off' if you want to. But it is still worth allowing your book to be published on Amazon – you never know, someone may be interested and want to buy it and it costs nothing.

Alternatively, if the book is very personal to you, you could simply delete it from Createspace after you have bought your personal copies, keeping your book exclusive to you.

When you set up your Createspace account make sure you fill in the section regarding payment of royalties. You can opt to have your payments made by direct transfer to your bank account or you can opt to be paid by cheque.

A Point to Note: If you list your book for general sale and live outside the US, Createspace will withhold 30% of your royalties until you have obtained a US tax number. A lot of countries have an agreement with US regarding royalties and, once you have your tax number, you will receive 100% of your royalties, depending on where you live.

Createspace have a section that will guide you through applying for your US tax number.

Also, if you have requested to be paid by cheque, depending

where you live, you should ask Createspace to withhold any royalty payments until you reach $100-150.

This is because a lot of non US banks charge quite a hefty fee for depositing a $ cheque – sometimes as much as half the check total.

For example, I'm told that in Australia, some banks charge $20Aus to deposit a US $ check. In UK it cost me around £6 if I pay a $US into my account.

So it makes sense, when you are just starting out, to let your royalties reach a level where the cheque won't be eaten up by bank charges.

After a couple of months, when you have a few books on Amazon and they are selling well, the royalty check should be more than enough to take you over the $100 limit.

Formatting Your Book

I am going to tell you how I format my books before uploading them.

There are lots of other ways to achieve the same thing, but this is the one that I find easiest – I am a bit technically challenged, so it has to be simple!

If I can do it, anyone can…

Once you are confident with this method of formatting your book, you could check out other ways to customize the size of your book.

The first thing you need to know is the size that you want your finished book to be. There are a number of standard industry trim sizes available from 5" x 8" to 8" x 10" and sizes in between.

Using a trim size outside of the industry standard will reduce your royalties because Createspace take a bigger percentage of each sale. It will also limit the possible online sales channels if you choose to upgrade to the ProPlan.

I use the 5.25" x 8" trim size for most of my books because it makes it easy to use a standard Word document for the draft.

To begin, open a Word document and write your working title. On your toolbar go to "Page Layout", from there choose the "Size" option.

Select **A5** in the dropdown menu. Your page(s) will be re-sized automatically.

You can re-size a completed book this way, but you must make sure you go through the whole thing carefully after you resize to make sure everything is positioned exactly how you want it.

Set the line spacing to 1.5 to make the book easier to read. I use 11pt and Arial font for my physical books; it is easy on the eye and looks good in print, but the choice is yours.

I always add a 'footer' to my physical books (but not Kindle books) which includes the book title, copyright and the author name and page number.

Click on the "Insert" tab on your toolbar and select "footer". Choose the format for your footer from the dropdown list. Write exactly what you want to appear at the bottom on every page. Centre it, then click "close" on the toolbar that popped up. Your footer should then appear at the bottom of each page.

Always add page numbers. Click "Insert" on your toolbar then "page numbers" on the dropdown menu.

Now you are ready to write your book.

Remember not to try and stuff too much on to one page – make it easy to read.

If you write "How to" books; you will only need to write one "tip" on each page.

Readers like to be able to skim the pages of a book to pick out the important points, so don't fill your book with irrelevant material.

But do make it look good.

Your book should be an *even* number of pages when finished.

If I finish on an odd page I usually add an extra page after the last page with an appropriate quote and perhaps a relevant photograph.

If you are including a "Contents" page leave it until after you have completely finished your book.

It saves you so much time if you are not keep going back and changing it every time you add or delete something that changes the page numbers.

Some authors leave their "Contents" page blank until after they have received their proof copy. They would proofread the book; then add a contents page before ordering a second proof copy.

However, if I am including a contents page, I prefer to submit a complete book including the contents page.

The best place for your contents is page 3. It looks much

better than being on the reverse side of the title page.

Page 1 would be your title page; page 2 could be an appropriate quote and picture or even a place for acknowledgements. This will mean that your "contents" page will be on the right hand side of your book when you open it (page 3). Page 4 could be a nice picture or a bit about the author so that first page of your book is also on the right hand side (page 5).

This is how I do it but you may want to do it differently.

Where to Get Photographs for your Book

Adding photographs or illustrations to your book will make it much easier on the eye and interesting for the reader.

If you are good at drawing then that is great – do your own illustrations. If you are good at photography use your own photographs.

But if like me, you are hopeless at anything remotely artistic you could use the royalty free photograph sites.

I use www.istockphotos.com for most of my photographs. But there are lots more royalty free photograph sites available online. Do a search and choose a site that appeals to you.

Remember to check the license details for any picture you use. Some photos are only licensed for personal use whilst others are for commercial use.

You would pay around $1-$2 for each photograph. There are photographs on even the most diverse of subjects.

You would only need smallest size available for most books.

Note: If you want to display your photos in full colour, it will considerably reduce your royalty on that book because it would obviously cost Createspace more to produce a full colour book.

I usually insert the colour photo then click on it and choose 'greyscale' rather than 'automatic' which is the default. Your photograph then will appear in black and white for print.

Below are some of my books, published using the Createspace method and the Createspace cover creator.

Note: You can use a pen name rather than your own name if you prefer.

Uploading Your Book to Createspace

Once you have written your book and are happy with the way it looks when you view it in the 'preview' section of your toolbar, it is time to turn the draft into a .pdf file to upload to Createspace.

This is the only type of file that is acceptable.

Please let me repeat this.

Do remember that Createspace will only print EXACTLY what you upload, they will not change ANYTHING.

So be *absolutely sure* that you have checked that everything is properly aligned and proofed before you convert to .pdf and upload it.

It is really simple to convert your files to .pdf. First you should save a copy of your Word file and store it in a folder so you will always have your original source files.

Next open your file and click on 'file' then 'save as'. Choose the .pdf option in the dropdown menu then click 'save'.

See below:

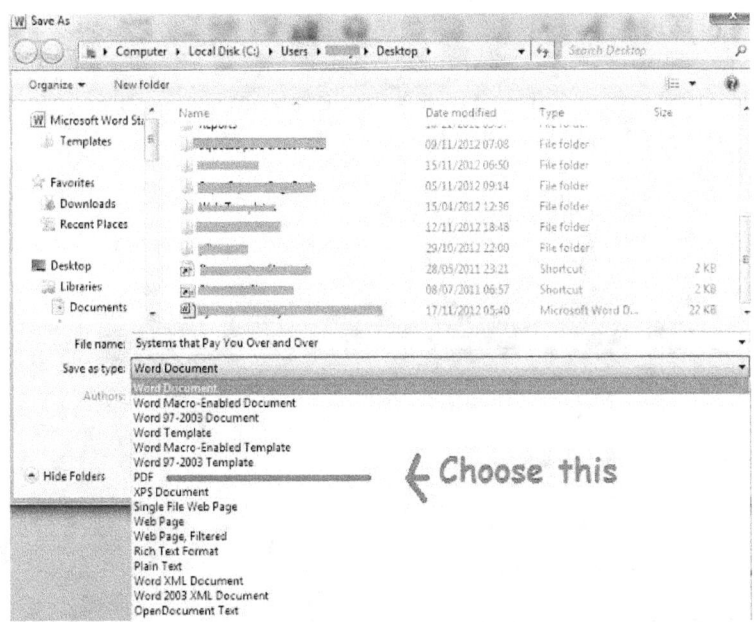

Your .pdf should open in your window. Check it over carefully.

You now have your interior files correctly formatted for Createspace.

Uploading your Files

Go to Createspace and sign in to the account that you created earlier. Click on "Add a New Title".

Two options will appear, Expert or Guided

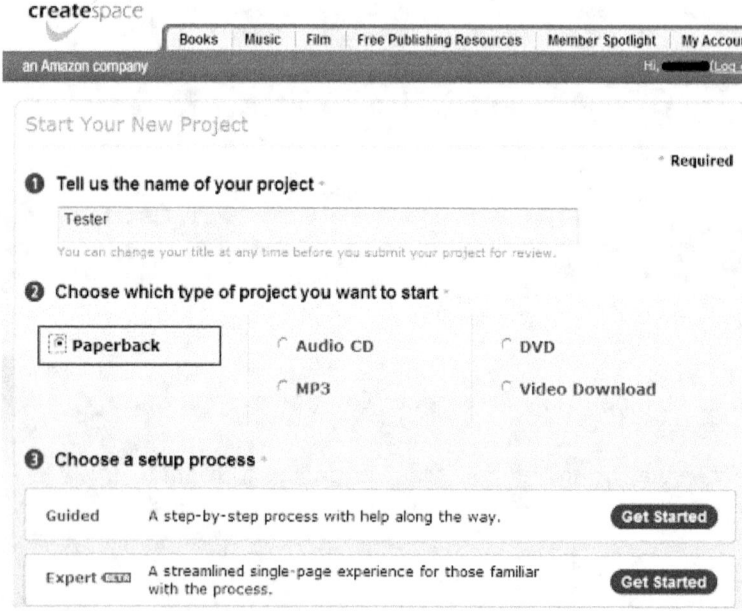

For your first few times it would be easier to use the 'Guided' section.

Click on the 'Get Started' button.

You will be asked for some details about your book.

- Title
- Subtitle
- Description – **this will be displayed on your Amazon page, so make it good**.
- ISBN – International Standard Book Number is a unique 10 or 13 digit number assigned to every book that identifies its binding, edition and publisher. ISBNs are obtained from R.R. Bowker, the US ISBN agency, or the International ISBN Agency. You can also have an ISBN assigned by Createspace (I do – it's free).
- Category Etc.

Fill this in as completely as you can. Click 'Save' at the bottom of the page.

You will be taken to the next section which asks about the physical properties of your book.

- Price – you decide what selling price to want to set. However, there is a minimum charge before you begin to accrue royalties – so check the minimum price for your size book.

- Trim Size

- Number of Pages

- Paper Colour.

Fill this in and click 'Save' at the bottom of the page.

The next section is where you will upload your interior pages i.e. your .pdf file.

Upload your file as per the simple instructions. You will then have to wait until you receive an email from Createspace confirming that your files are correctly formatted for the trim size that you selected.

If you are using the 5.25" x 8" trim and A5 page size, it should be fine.

Creating your Book Cover

The next step is to create your book cover.

There are **3** ways to accomplish this.

1. If you are good at graphics, you can do it yourself using Photoshop and the cover template supplied on Createspace – sadly this method is currently beyond my technical capabilities.

2. Pay someone to do it for you. There are hundreds, if not thousands of graphic designers who can do this for you. It should cost around $20 for a very good book cover.

Check out websites like www.warriorforum.com and look in their classified section. You will find lots of very talented people who will design a beautiful cover exactly as you want it.

Ask for examples of work before agreeing to work with anyone to make sure that you are happy with the quality that they have done previously.

Make sure that you find someone who has had experience in creating these types of book covers as they need to be in a format acceptable to Createspace.

You should also remember to tell them to leave a space in the design for the barcode.

Another place to buy a very reasonably priced book cover ($5) design is at www.fiverr.com but really take the time to investigate the people offering to do the job – some are fantastic, others are not so good.

Again, you need to see samples of previous book covers that they have produced.

For some of my books I use a graphic designer, others I use the third option – it's easy and free.

3. Use one of the many ready formatted templates that are provided on Createspace to design your own cover. There are lots of different designs to choose from that you can edit to your own preference.

You can add photos, change fonts and colours, add author photos and an author bio along with a brief description of your book.

I sometimes add a second photograph to the back cover instead of the author photo.

Most books with less than 120 pages are spineless, which means that you won't have the author name and title running down the spine of your book.

If you have created your book cover with the Createspace tool, you simply click on "Save" to submit your finished design.

However, if you have created your own cover or had someone do it for you, you will have to convert it to a .pdf file as you did with your interior pages before you upload it.

When you have uploaded the files, you will have to wait for an email to tell you that your files have been approved.

Once both sections, interior pages and cover, have been approved you should order a proof copy to check that everything is as you want it to be.

This will cost around $4 plus shipping.

You will get another email to tell you that your proof copy has been sent.

When the proof copy arrives, go through it very carefully to make sure that everything is as it should be.

If there are changes to be made you will have to amend your files, convert to .pdf and upload to Createspace as before.

You should purchase another proof copy to check your changes.

If however, your book is exactly as you want it to be, log into your account at Createspace and check the box that says 'Publish'.

That's it - Congratulations - you are now a Published Author and for a miniscule outlay – your book will be available on Amazon within a few days.

You need not do anything more with that book but, if you want to sell lots of copies on Amazon and make money, it may be a good idea to see if you can get some reviews for it.

Prospective buyers will usually read the reviews to find out if the book is worth buying.

You could ask your family and friends to buy it and leave a review.

You could go to forums related to your book subject and offer a copy of your book (obviously a downloadable copy rather than a physical one) in exchange for a review.

You could also visit the 'Book Review' community section on the Createspace website where you can offer a copy of your book for review in exchange for reviewing their books.

Join the communities on Amazon and look for discussions about how to get genuine reviews.

Make sure that any reviews that you solicit are genuine and honest. Amazon will take a dim view of any false reviews

Never pay money for reviews; it is against Amazon's terms and conditions and could result in your account being banned – it has happened!

If you want to earn a residual income from your self-publishing, it's time to 'rinse and repeat' – so get to it and write your next book.

Remember, the more books that you have on Amazon; the more passive income you could generate.

The very best thing about this form of self-publishing is

- Amazon is a hugely popular website, getting over **42 million visits** per month.

- You don't have to deal with any stock – Amazon will do that.

- You don't have to market your book – Amazon will do that. They have an email list of **gigantic** proportions.

- You don't have to collect any money – Amazon will do that.

- You don't have to deal with any mailing – Amazon will do that.

- You don't have to deal with refunds or customer service – Amazon will do that.

Your book will be available on Amazon for years to come without you having to do anything else at all.

You simply wait for the cheques to arrive each month.

However, if you spend time promoting your book you could considerably increase your sales.

Consider sending a free copy along with a press release to your local newspaper. This could be a good local interest story for them and you will get lots of exposure for your book.

You can order some of your own books at the proof price and take them to local bookshops and ask if they would be interested in stocking it on their shelves

Research other ways to promote your book; there are lots of websites that will give you some good ideas.

Section 3

Publishing your Book for the Kindle Reader

Digital books

Under the Amazon Kindle Direct Publishing program, anyone with a great story or content to share can effortlessly create their very own books to sell on Amazon Kindle, earning up to 70% royalties along the way – much more than Createspace.

Contrary to what you may think, this is a very easy process. Not only that, there is no limit to the subject matter, which means that you can publish lots of books on various topics in order to maximize your earnings.

For example if you publish one book and you could get around 100 sales per month. Now imagine if you increase your offering to several books – say 10-20.

Not only are there no additional fees and considering that digital books are a one-time investment, meaning you only have to create a digital book once, you could quickly recover any initial investment such as the cover design, and make a nice profit as well.

If you intend to publish books in a few different genres, you could use pen names to keep the subjects separate. This helps to establish you as 'expert' in a particular genre.

Kindle publishing is very easy compared to the real-world hassles of having to sell your manuscript to publishing houses or persuading publishing agents sign you up as one of their authors.

In fact, it is so easy that almost anyone can do it.

Publishing your Work on Amazon Kindle

Before beginning to write your book, the very first decision to make would be the topic. You may want to publish your Family Legacy on Kindle or your Family Recipe Book, or you may have lots of other ideas.

When trying to figure out what to write about, you could consider the seasons. For example, just before the holiday seasons, it would be good to write about any of the following:

Christmas

- Gift Buying Tips
- Decorating Tips
- Holiday Do-it-Yourself Guides (such as DIY Christmas gifts, DIY Christmas Decors)
- Dishes to Serve on Christmas Eve
- Baking ideas for Christmas.

New Year

- How to Celebrate the New Year
- New Year Gift-Giving
- Crafts
- Party Ideas
- New Year Resolutions

Valentines Day

- Dating Tips

- Romantic Baking Ideas
- Top Dating Restaurants (in the form of a review)
- Dishes to serve
- Romantic gift Ideas

Halloween

- Original Costume ideas
- Spooky Party Food
- Party Themes

As you may know, demand for reading resources usually increases just before a particular season but there are many other topics that you can write about whatever the season.

Sex and Relationships, Health and Well-being, Yoga, Meditation, Food, Self Help topics, Diet and even Technology are just a few of the more popular subjects.

Amazon's Bestseller List

Another great way to get some inspiration is to check Amazon's Bestseller's list.

Writing an Information or 'How to' digital book

If you are going to write informational books, once you have decided on a topic it's time to get some writing done. This is my blueprint for writing an information book in the shortest time possible.

An age-old proven format for writing an information based book is:

1. **Tell them what you are going to tell them (*Introduction*)**

2. **Tell them (*Body of book*)**

3. **Tell them what you have told them (Conclusion)**

The Title

Choose something that is interesting and catches the eye. In most cases it is the title and book cover that sells the book to a prospective purchaser.

If you are writing about Training your Dog, try using something like:

"15 Simple Secrets for Training your Dog that Every Frustrated Dog Owner Should Know"

or

"The Idiots Guide to Training your Idiot Dog"

(I'm going to use that one for my next Dog book!)

Your potential reader will be more likely to check out your book if the title promises something different, **so be creative**.

Remember to include the keywords in the title (the words that people may type into the Amazon search bar when looking for a book – in this case, Training your Dog).

Writing Your Book

1. Write the Introduction

Write the introduction to your book. Use three or four paragraphs outlining what the book is about and why they need to read it.

In the introduction always remember to tell your prospective reader exactly how the book will help them and what benefits they are likely to get from your book.

2. Body

Write a *list of relevant topics* that you want to cover in your book – these will be your chapters. Begin the list with the first topic that you will write about and then progress *logically* through to the conclusion. You can always change stuff around later if you need to.

Now take each topic and write a few paragraphs about it. Six or seven hundred words for each topic is about right – but that is up to you. You should write as many words as it takes to explain each topic fully.

3. Conclusion

Write your conclusion and reiterate exactly what the reader has learned.

Finally, add the legal stuff; copyright and disclaimers.

The final step is to proofread and edit your book.

Do this once when you have finished it, then put it away for at least three days.

Now proofread and edit one more time – it's amazing the small mistakes you can find that you missed the first time round.

Even a low priced digital book should be your very best work.

There you have it, a simple step-by-step method to writing any information based book.

Designing the Cover for Your Book

One of the things that can help sales when releasing your book would be the cover.

For a digital product, the customer doesn't really see much of the product. So, it is important that you convince your customer not only with the content but with how the product looks – in this case, the book cover. Don't forget they will not have the opportunity to pick up your book and flick through the pages to check if it is what they want.

To help in designing your book cover, I have prepared a short list of things to consider that could help increase your conversion rates.

Be clear about what the book is all about. Whilst design is a very important part of the book, you should also remember that your customers are looking for information – and they have to know that the information they are looking for is found in your book.

Don't forget to include the name of the author. This may not exactly be much help to the new Kindle publisher. However once you have created a name for yourself in the business, having your name appear on the cover would help increase the book's authority. Even if you're a new writer, this can also be an advantage to you – it could even be the first step to creating a name for yourself within your chosen genre (branding).

Use a Bold Colour. Amazons pages are white, so use a colour for your cover that will stand out.

Use a Flat Cover – not a 3D cover that you would use for an ebook.

Check out how bestselling authors design their covers for Amazon.

Do they use specific colours and fonts in your genre?

Is there a particular format that appeals to you?

Use what you can see is already working. Not the exact same cover but the general feel of the cover.

Formatting and Uploading your Book to Kindle

Save your book file in the correct format.

When using Word to write your book, make sure that you choose the A5 page size and set all your margins to 1.00.

A couple of other things to take note of when you're preparing your material for Kindle:

- The best fonts to use are the simple ones. I use Verdana 12pt and 1.0 line spacing for all my Kindle books.

- The simpler the format, the better it is. People reading on their Kindles or other devices for that matter, are looking for great content not jazzy design.

- If you need a page break, insert it manually through the Word toolbar. If you just hit return Kindle leaves a white space rather than starting a new page as you intended.

- Allow your text to run on through your pages as you type. Remember this is digital publishing, so the rules are different than publishing physical books.

- It is also is worth mentioning that people who will buy your digital books will be reading your content on devices no bigger than half the size of your laptop's screen. So, bear that in mind when formatting your book.

- If you're planning to wrap text around an image, you may want to check whether or not the text has actually wrapped around the image – or if it has been bumped to the next page (personally, I never wrap text around a picture – it saves hassle).

Save a copy of your book to your desktop, then open the copy and go to 'File' then 'save as'. Save the file as 'Webpage, filtered'.

See Below:

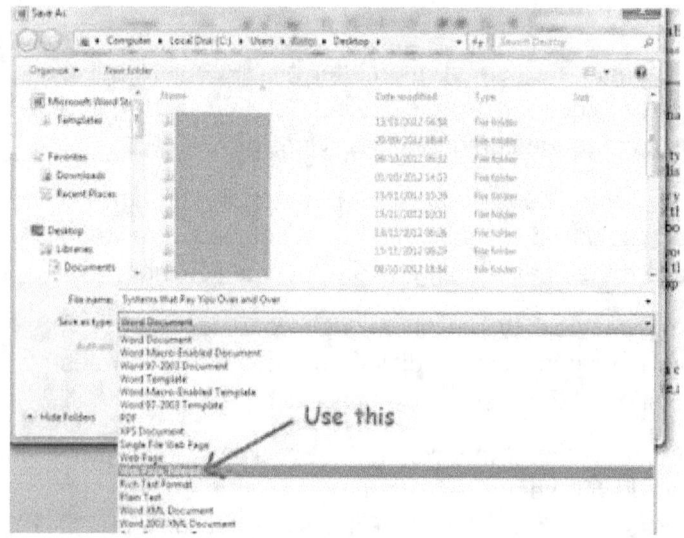

IMPORTANT

If your book contains pictures you will see that when you have saved your file as 'Webpage filtered' two sections appear on your desktop. One is a folder containing all your pictures; the other is the filtered webpage.

In order to make your pictures show up in the Kindle reader you should:

Create a new folder on your desktop and move the two sections to the folder. It doesn't work if you simply add your filtered webpage to the picture folder.

Give the new folder a name then save to a .zip file.

The .zip file is the one that you will upload to Kindle.

Download the free ebook reader so you can check out how your book will appear on the Kindle. If the book doesn't appear as you would like it to, make notes so you remember what to change.

You can make the necessary changes before uploading it to Kindle.

Create an Amazon Account

Go to Amazon.com and you should be greeted by a login screen. If you don't have an account yet, all you have to do would be to enter your email address and pick the option, "No, I am a new customer" and the select "Sign in using our secure server".

Register with Amazon's Kindle Direct Publishing

The next step requires you to set up your Kindle Publishing account. Scroll to the bottom of Amazon's home page and click the link as below:

Before you upload your book file, you have to first agree to the terms of service by clicking on the "Agree" button.   After agreeing to the terms, you will be required to enter additional information such as Name, Address, Country and the option by which you opt to receive your royalties.

After you've filled out the form, click on the save button at the bottom right of the page.

Amazon will save your information and you will be notified with "**Your account information has been successfully saved**".

Next, click on "BOOKSHELF" at the top of the page.

Uploading your Digital Book

Remember: Before you upload your first book, download the free Kindle Previewer so you can check out how your book will appear on the Kindle if you haven't already done it. You will find this next to the 'upload file' option. If the book doesn't appear as you would like it to, you can make the necessary changes before uploading it to your 'Bookshelf'

Now it's time to actually upload your book. On the Bookshelf, click "ADD NEW TITLE".

There are tooltips provided for almost every field. If you are uncertain about what they are for, click on the fields respective "WHAT'S THIS?" link and the further explanation will be provided.

When filling in the 'description' field, remember that this is your 'sales' copy. So make it good. This section and the book cover will help persuade the 'browser' to become a buyer.

At the bottom of the page, you will be required to upload your book file and Amazon will convert it to its Kindle format automatically. Please be patient as upload time depends on the size of your book file and your internet speed.

You will be taken to the next step of the process where you will be required to enter additional information.

When setting the price for your book, remember that 70% royalties are only available if your book is between $2.99 and $9.99. The royalty is 30% for any other price point.

After you have satisfactorily completed the information required, you will be returned to the 'bookshelf' with your book in the queue.

Note: Your book will say "in review" as its status. As a policy, Amazon reviews all content submitted to them. English content takes up to 24 hours, with other languages taking 2 to 3 days. This is part of Amazon's effort to strengthen the Kindle experience and ensure high quality among all its products.

If you would like to read more about this, you may click the "What's this?" link under the status on the page.

You can change the price, title and description of your books at any time. Just click on the link form your 'Bookshelf' then edit the fields required and click 'save'.

Don't delete the book and republish as you will lose any ranking that you may have achieved. It will still go into the 'in review' status but you keep any rankings.

Marketing your Book

It is no good simply writing and uploading your book to Kindle then sitting and waiting for the sales to flood in – it won't happen.

You may be lucky and get a few sales but, if you want your book to be listed on Amazon's bestsellers list you have to do some promotion.

There are lots of Kindle groups on Facebook that you could join. Most of these are really helpful for beginners as you would usually find quite a few members that are willing to share their expertise with a newcomer.

Marketing your book is outside the scope of 'Your Family Legacy' so head over to Amazon and join some of the Kindle communities (there is a link at the top of your 'Bookshelf' page). There is lots of useful information and lots of helpful people available there.

My final thoughts:

Nothing will be achieved if you simply read this book and do nothing.

Make a pledge to yourself to get at least one book published on Amazon Kindle or Createspace to test out your new skills. It doesn't have to be perfect, you can always re-do it later once you have got the hang of it.

I look forward to hearing about your success.

Take Action Now!

If you have any questions about formatting your book for Createspace or Kindle, or would like me to proofread, edit or even simply upload your manuscript or create your cover at competitive rates, send an email to:

ljs@iwantd.com

I am a fully qualified copy editor and proof-reader and have a number of books that I have successfully self-published.

Finally, the small print

It is prohibited to reproduce any part of this book in any form unless agreed in writing by the author and it is only intended for the personal use of the purchaser. Anyone found contravening the copyright laws will be prosecuted to the fullest extent of the law.

Whilst examples of potential earnings may be included – I take no responsibility for the earnings of others.

Your own efforts will determine your eventual results.

"*I like books that aren't just lovely but that have memories in themselves. Just like playing a song, picking up a book again that has memories can take you back to another place or another time.*" ~ **Emma Watson**